CityRandom-RandomCity Presents:

# <u>Moon Rocks</u>

## The Creative Writings of Big Bo$$ Rhino

By: Franklin "FreeMan" Cabell

Moon Rocks: The Creative Writings of Big Bo$$ Rhino

ISBN-10: 0-692-13977-X

ISBN-13: 978-0-692-13977-6

## *Haiku*

Inspiration is
found in **EVERYTHING!** Create
effective platforms...

*"Sipped a pint of mutagen the secret of the ooze,*

*DNA and molecules got mixed up and infused.*

*Mutated into something better than what I*

*was used to. Can withstand anything, what it is,*

*what it do?"*

**-Big Bo$$ Rhino**

# P R E F A C E:

## A Word From A FreeMan

After GOD, I thank YOU for your time, open minds and reading eyes...

My name is Frank, and I am a FreeMan!

This collection of poems, songs, haiku and rhyming monologues are metaphorical rocks (intentionally formatted as an out of sequence story) that I use as projectiles to throw at the moon. The moon in this context represents a few things. One being that the sky's the limit. Focus on something in the universe that you can see (mentally or physically), set a goal, aim high and when you get there, aim higher! The other represents something in the universe that orbits you. Something that won't go away or easily let you go.

Or things you have trouble with letting go of yourself. Things, people and/or situations you may have a hard time dealing with, knowing of, or being a part of it's existence. What it is, what it was and what it may or may not become next. The latter is where most of these "rocks" (whatever was on my mind at the time of writing) are being thrown.

I

If I hit my target, cool! But if not, I still aimed high and it's all in the universe somewhere and off of my mind, so that's cool too. Hence the title

"Moon Rocks."

This project also serves as the proverbial burial site of a lot of thought processes and ideas I've had that may be revisited from time to time to place flowers on. The content of this book is inspired by an extremely peculiar time in my life. GOD was made visible and HE took and required a lot from me. It was HE who decided it was time I got OG checked while letting me know who's really in charge. I prayed on EVERYTHING... a lot!

Of all the things I prayed for, HE decided to restore my then lost ability to put words together to form songs, poetry or whatever form of creative writing or media I use to tell my tale. It's a reason why he saw fit to bring these things back and forced me to let go of others, but HIS plan is perfect and I have to trust it... as hard as that is. It's strange to actually receive the things you ask for through him. It's not always neat, pretty or the most vividly painted picture placed right in front of you, but if you really take the time to put things into perspective, you'll get your answers and discover positive solutions. For that I'm thankful and can say I'm truly blessed. HE sends us struggles and hard times to strengthen us for HIS glory.

It took me a while to understand what that really means, but now I get it.

With honor and love, I'd like to thank my mom. I'd hate to sound cliché, but without her having my back, I don't know where I'd be in this world, thanks for being you! Thanks to my big brother Booby for always telling me to pray on everything and worry about nothing. That's probably the most solid advice anyone has ever given me, thank you. My three first brovacuzinz Die Hard Da C'zar, Jym Stryka and ChrisIs... y'all ignant yet wise ass geniuses! Anytime I needed y'all, you three would always come through and go hard every single time with no questions asked. You three are the living definition of the saying "blood is thicker than water", thank you for always looking out for this runt! DB, if my mama had a third child, it'd definitely be you. Thanks for having a leveled head and never changing! Chillz D. Monolo, thanks for pushing me to work when I didn't have it in me to do so, being honest, and supportive of whatever project I was working on at any given time. D, thanks for coming through in a clutch! You've always helped me to stay focused and meet deadlines, thanks, brah! Smoke... asshole... nuff said... thanks for being just that brah. There's one in every family, salud! TChaosItself and Bunmi, words can't describe how thankful I am for the wisdom you two have shared with me. Thank you very much!

Reign, somewhere in this vast and ever expanding universe, and if I believed they existed, you'd be my soulmate. Never change for anything or anyone and thanks for being the great, inspirational and motivational person that you are! Booga and Cee Jay, thanks for always telling it like it is and praying for and with me. Mayo, thanks for always supporting me and actually showing up. If nobody else ever says it, I'm proud of you, brova! Jusme, thanks for being an inspirational figure and driving force that reintroduced me to this world of poetry, and also providing a venue. It's truly an honor to know you!

There's a metric ton of others that I'd like to name and give a reason why I'm thanking them, but that list would make this part of the book stupidly longer than what it needs to be. Also I'd be thanking some people for showing me who they REALLY are. Though I'm thankful for you and everything you've done for and/or to me (pick one… or both), I'm sure you wouldn't want your names mentioned in that context. So by all means, if your conscious allows you to feel that the shoe fits... anywhosawhateverummm... all of you (named and unnamed) inspire me to do better and motivate my attempts at GREATNESS, I love you all!

By reading this book, maybe you'll learn a little bit about me, be inspired, find something here that you can relate to (or not) and/or just simply be entertained. That part's up to you to decide. I've rambled long enough as I have a tendency to do at times. So again, thanks for your time and blessing me with the opportunity to share these words with you. It really means a lot to me. Enjoy!

Glory to GOD and peace be with you KINGS and QUEENS, It's CityRandom, G'aiight!

## Table of Contents

## Chapter One:

### Incoherent Gibberish

In this chapter you'll find a bunch of sporadic ideas and random concepts where I mostly followed my pen to see where it'd take me.

-3-

VII

## Chapter Two:

### The Exclusive Recluse

The poems, rhyming monologues and songs of this chapter are documented thoughts and conversations that I've had with myself.

-23-

## Chapter Three:

### Tape Deck Playlist

A musically influenced trip into my world through
my ever changing and open ear to music.

-49-

## Chapter Four:

## PROpul(l)SHUN

The content of this chapter include pieces based on prayers, introspective moments that I've had and reminders of what I already have and know of within.

-73-

X

### _Haiku_

Maybe today's the

new day that I spoke about

a lil while ago...

Chapter One:

## Incoherent Gibberish

In this chapter you'll find a bunch of sporadic ideas and random concepts where I mostly followed my pen to see where it'd take me. Some make sense while others may not as much, but it's all creative expression... right?

# L7 Zero

Ain't no more taking scraps from nonbelievers,
bogus leaders opened my eyes to see hidden
deceivers.

Fake like I'm needed but bleeded for resources,
selfish alternate motives, loyalty out the window
from folks I thought was the closest.

Notice it ain't no love lost or ill will to anybody, not
a second thought about any shoddy party.

Self-reliance obtained after revelations within, real
and fake don't blend, opposite definition of... friend.

I rep myself and that's a power move. If ever
disappointed worth to myself is all I have to prove.

My new beginning starts at zero, number one will
follow soon. Plotting my journey to the surface of the
moon.

## Play-Doh & Legos

If somewhere in the universe I was blessed with the divine power of making things from nothing into existence, what a mess it'd be that I'd create. Too much of an internal debate of how to handle something of that magnitude and weight is much too great.

Do I have the imagination to create the things we as people take for granted? Such as grass, trees, the sea, rock and the soil in which these things are planted?

Ecosystems and organisms, microcosms, grand scale or not so vital. All designed to unify and sustain through whatever I allow, and elements I bring to rival.

The creativity to create a human-like form from the Earth we'd stand and walk upon, be able to guide, lead and all knowing enough to show and tell them the way that things should be run?


Would I walk amongst or rule above? Iron fist or rubber glove? Display and have true unconditional love for who and what does what it does?

Natural selection or unlimited protection? Monotone or different complexions? All the same or different sections of things my humanity sees in it's own reflection?

Even the will or ability to influence the beings of this said planet, might look to me frustrated and panicked when the life I've provided get's too out of hand to manage.

I'd never promise a perfect world, but it's made as beautifully as I could make it. Try to be rational with it all let and nothing corrupt the power that I've tasted.

Not being thoughtless or blasphemous or saying I could do GOD's work better, if anything I'm thankful and humbled by his ability and grace to hold and put all things together.

Too much pressure and a job for any human so why bother trying to be, just know your place and seek the face of he who brings you peace.

## Bouq & Hennessey

As I fidget spin this fidget spinner, sip my liquor by the hitter, buzzed but straight my liver withers, makes her look better and want them digits... quicker.

Silhouette of a fine frame in feminine form. Start off cold, talk makes her warm... up to the ideas and rhetoric I speak suggestively while staying cool as a fan unlike these busy body niggas after her hive in a swarm.

Casually conversing to peak perversions, words bounce back and forth from person to person.

Ideas exchange as the tab rapidly rises. Been my self whole time, no need to lead under false pretense or disguises.

Really... I'm focused on this drink I'm nursing... but companies cool, so... ain't no thirsting.

Just by chance we're in the same place at the same time. That's gotta count for or mean something, right? Tell her... "you could stay or leave or come with me... to see where goes this night."

At this point my heads a blender, so if I'm too forward, excuse what I think is charm. It's all playful banter no offense to be taken cause I really mean to you no harm.

I'll close the tab, tip the bartender and we can finish these cups, the next play is your call, so ummm... yeah, what ups?

## The Face

All about her anatomy, eyes staring deeply into mine.
Head bobbing like the beat was tight trying to find a
place to start her rhyme.

Counting bars between the verse and hook, freestyle
put away the book. Cause she's coming off top
showing true skill it's a talent head bang ballad off
her cleansed pallet.

But I like the way the flow switch, raw spit through
her pop filter. Hand gestures show emphasis, word
play she's a lyricist.

Punctuation and annunciation all factors when it
comes to this. Got it right on the first take, no
mistakes or a word missed.

Metaphors and action verbs, come to life when they
pass her lips. Rock the mic like it's effortless, hard
worker no rest in this.

Prove to me you the best at this. Top my charts first
on my list. In or on your face, answer now, are you
down for this?

## Inhibited Counterparts

How many times are you gonna tell me you don't
care about what makes me tic? How many times
must I hear it before it sticks?

Out of the same mouth that says "I love you", comes
some of the most vile, despicable, hateful, ungrateful,
lewd things I've ever heard spewed.

I know the game, hurt me before I again hurt you.
My efforts to be better can't stand alone because it
takes two.

The way you feel isn't totally your fault... but if I
bring kindness, decency and a degree of urgency to
make an honest attempt to make up for time past
should reap at least some benefit.

Let you have your way until it's just too much, I'd
rather chill than fuss and cuss about things of old and
what would kill our progress towards other much
better stuff... ENOUGH!!!

## Free Or Sumfin'...

Free in thought, free in theory, free in all that I hold dearly.

Free to fly free to fail, free to navigate this ship I sail.

Can't control wind direction or the way the current flows, but work in unison with it's motions to keep this ship afloat.

Free to succeed, free to win, free to go out on a whim.

Free to compete, fit in or dare to be different. Free to keep it moving on to something distant.

Gears are shifting while turning pistons give power to propel this engine, peak performance is non conformance that keeps oppressors cringing...

## Anti-AmurriKKKan

I's a coon, I's a nigger, I's a jiggaboo. Jungle bunny,
tar baby, black is beautiful.

Porch monkey, a gallowog, nignog. Blue gum,
boogie, niglet the list goes on...

These are the slurs, stereotypes, epithets and
disrespect spoon fed to my face... not cool. But, I
embrace the fear of me and of what I'm capable, so...
Thank you.

But on to this blindfolded, peckerwood bitch with the
scales... bless her heart... Probably weighing meth or
coke or whatever unnatural dope that keeps them
fueled by whatever dreams they sell you so... Be
smart.

But they trust that bitch's theory though, live and die
by it. Better yet they manipulate that shit, twist what
she's supposed to represent.

In the pursuit of what that other tall blue burning
bitch in New York stands for amongst other things,
or that cracked ass bell in Philly that probably could
never ring.

13

At least not for me. Not for my kind, not on my line not for us in what's considered to be the darkies of this so called vast minority.

It's like... Fuck the contributions made by those who look like me. To benefit this world and could improve our way of life within this degenerate society.

Scratch a lie find a thief, peel an orange and make it chief, kick up some shit, illegitimate beef, white wash bleach, rinse, repeat.

In these streets people get red, white and blued on. More bullshit every time you turn the tube on. From crisis actors to Kickstart backers  that's the news that get's abused that keeps this country separate and torn.


Distracted by... What's the hot topic now? World War 3? Scandalous athletes? Bogus reality TV, celebrities? Selfish greed and not the needs of those who live in poverty.

Not supposed to be conscious or pay that much attention though. Because it's online and on social media so... That makes it so.

Of the people, for the people, whatever they say or talk about. Just try not to become the next hashtag or victim of something whenever stepping out.

Not seeking approval nor worried bout being
welcome at their table. Not for me. But in they're
eyes all they see... Unfortunately... Is that...


I's a coon, I's a nigger, I's a jiggaboo. Jungle bunny,
tar baby, black is beautiful.

Porch monkey, a gallowog, nignog. Bluegum,
boogie, niglet the list goes on.

# Why! (Part One)

Back into my artwork spent a minute off the bracket,
I ain't seen it neither but it's presence here was never
absent.

Worlds crashed collided like my Chally hit that
Civic, overcast clearing up to him the thanks I have
to give it.

I'm living and I've never felt more alive now's the
time, for me to organize I can see clearly now that
the tears dried.

I have a testimony, not yet, I'm still going through it,
clockwork motions the flow of things is so fluid.

Poster child of everything becoming full circle nah,
still a long road ahead I pray that I'm prepared.

A lot you find when you there or learn along the
path, simple math to a genius is easily out classed.

Test in life I try to pass it, flying colors, gold star, A
plus… but still I wonder.

Doubt has been eliminated, hurdles jumped over,
crossed the line of many breaking points I live my
life slower.

Maybe crawl to a standstill but how is that living?
Roll with the punches of anything that I'm given.

Scratch and bring to surface whatever it is that's
hidden, eyes, mind, heart and ears open, answer
please, I'm listening...


Why, I know Why so I don't ask why me, mind, heart
and eyes open was blind but now I see.

Thought I was trippin' and wasn't right mentally,
Epiphany, moment of clarity made whole instantly...

# G St. NW

The other day I made a friend in the most unlikely of places. We shared common interests like music and fine women with pretty faces.

But, the difference between he and I that makes this whole scenario far fetched, is that he's an ostrich.

With wings as wide as an office desk, and I'm about as tall as his neck.

He wears baseball caps, wife beaters, and skinny jeans every day of the week. He also wears flip flops as a cigarette hangs from his beak.

A political mind at best as he often discusses our economy. Ways to resolve and fix things up, including foreign policy.

How our government makes a mockery of our lower class, homeless and downtrodden, and how that war was more about oil, than it was ever about Bin Laden.

Tired of all the untruths, fibs, just flat out lies, conspiracies, cover ups and all of all kinds bogus replies.

That's why he moved away from here. With him he took his television, a PlayStation, the series of Metal Gear, Now and Laters and Newports, and an endless supply of beer.

About his home you ask? It's a place we all can see but we're nowhere near. His residence, the moon, in the largest crater, you'll see him when the night is clear.

Whenever I'm invited up to hang and smash off brews, he sends my way a candy purple, Buick Park Avenue.

It sounds like a vacuum and it's powered by weather balloons. With strippers filling every seat, and a trunk equipped with boom.

Don't worry about the atmosphere, it let's off eco-friendly fumes. As it zooms it reminds me of Altered Beast, when that dude says "welcome to your doom."

Strange thing is there's no need for oxygen, or even a space suit. No containment stations, only a place to regroup.

On the moon your problems seem to float away. Your yesterdays are less heavy, and nothing at all seams deadly, and the beer is always ready.

BUT DAMN THAT!!! I'm here with a big ass cigarette smoking, talking ostrich with clothes on!!! Cool as ever though, but between two worlds torn.

The party's over when it's over. Overloaded, plus not sober. Pulled the car onto the shoulder, we just hit that cow that's jumping over... The Moon.

# Rumination

Souvenirs from places foreign, highest height of
elevation soaring looking over carefully watching
where I'm going .

Long forgotten is myself and the places I reminisce
about. It may just be better that way. What's gone
today just let it stay where it is til memories become
vague.

Nonexistent even... Long overdue treatment to
regroup  from things I must lose while breathing.

The sun creates a glare to distort and bring
discomfort to those unaware of it's magnificence, a
celestial body who's beams I seek for energy given so
generous... ly.

No shade to throw, only to sit under to block rays of
ultra violence. Ten toes and two melanated legs but
still somewhat off balance.

Crawl, walk, faster, run, jump, fly. Hear, think, learn
open up my third eye.

…and grow. Endure what's possible, peace to what's
not, never wishing ill will but, leave it where it is to
rot... or not... whatever... g'aiight...

### *Haiku*

My tough skin leaves me

unable to feel, see or

recognize most things...

Chapter Two:

## The Exclusive Recluse

The poems, rhyming monologues and songs of this chapter are documented thoughts and conversations that I've had with myself. Also it's a short, incomplete tour of the shallowness and depths of a battlefield known as "Franklin's Head." A place where every conflict is acknowledged and addressed.

## The Middle Child Blues

Second in one family, last in another, first only to
me. Some call it jealousy, but I argue sibling rivalry.

Self made from birth on this road I've paved. I mean,
you won't believe the shade these eyes have seen.
From leftovers, table scraps to hand me downs,
through it all I've never been green.

Fighting for attention I sit back wishing my brothers
would give me the time ever of day or even mention.
Maybe listen to what I'm pitching instead of
dismissing... me.

I'm a perfect storm of all combined. Slept on by
everybody, even them. Too tall to look up to my big
brother so I don't even bother him.

My little brother looks down on me. Self-conscious
and I feel that he frowns on me, but... that's my
family.

Calamity in this scatterbrain, against the grain I'm all
terrain. Rebellious to this world I claim... so through
it all I don't complain.

Dysfunctional in the same ways as many. When it
comes to love, I dish out plenty. While not expecting,
I'm giving freely but when my turn comes around...
there's hardly any...

Ride the bench nah, I play the fence while dealing with these incidents. It makes no sense it get's like this but… that's the way it is.

## Bipolarizedificationifiedationesslydomisment (Misdiagnosed, Self Medicated)

This FreeMan don't have a free hand to offer free shit to anybody… Not anymore… been free thrown away and free fell and free flown and to obliteration been free blown.

Dumped off in murky waters, y'all heard bout what happened to Rivers… or did you? let's just say he's on vacation, moving along, anywho...

To give a free fuck... just might be too much, so I try to act as such but backfires like the pipes on an old ass truck.

I don't wanna care about nothing no more. Ain't sore bout nothing to do about nothing or everything or anything these nerves of mine find unsettling.

Seems that all I have is me, and I'm under the impression that's how it's supposed to be. This tapestry of fuckery I see won't leave me be so easily.

To end this train wreck in progress, I look above for context. Pray for what I need before I knot the bow that tightens up my Stotches. (boots)

If it wasn't for bad luck, I guess I'd have none at all. Whatever way the dice fall how they may is how you crap out or continue to play them after they bounce back off the wall.

The decision making process of going for broke for things you're not so sure of, has the ability to be overwhelming to say the least but worthwhile if you find peace.

I'm still searching for mine... I guess it'll get here when it get's here. To be real clear I'm a passenger in this ride... Lord? Please take the wheel... steer...

# The Wizzurrrd

Is it wrong that, I'm that grown assed man who, gets off work like it's school and, gets off work like it's school and, fixes a bowl of cereal and…

Sits on the couch or edge of the bed, in my underwear, my underwear, on the couch or edge of the bed… after a shower to clear my head?

Probably not… I just be chillin', configure my controller to defeat the villain.

All the King Koopas, Troopers, Goombas and Dr. Wilys and Robotnics... get crushed by Mario, Rock and Sonic.

Achievements and trophies for resourceful weapon making, bravely I showed Joel how to lead Ellie to safety.

Donkey Kong ain't got nuffin' on me! Most of my adventures take place on a 60 inch screen.

From kid to teen to now adult, still got all my systems in my vault.

Old to the most recent ones I bought. Handheld portables notable on the go, "gotta catch em' all" is what I was taught.

Navigate the maze until I get caught. Make it to the end to do battle with Onslaught.

Waited outside in line for new releases. Collected Amiibo for physical pieces.

"It's so bad" when I'm "Playing With Power", I get "Welcomed To The Next Level" where "Greatness Awaits", then I "Jump In" to where I "Play It Louder".

Different genres and play styles keep stories interesting, if you ain't hip, take initiative to learn something bout what it is you missing... game on...


Is it wrong that, I'm that, grown assed man who, gets off work like it's school and, gets off work like it's school and, fixes a bowl of cereal and...

Sits on the couch or the edge of the bed, in my underwear, my underwear, on the couch or edge of the bed... after a shower to clear my head?

# Mirror Talk

Frank, get your shit together! If you still trippin' over
that bitch, man burgerbass whatever.

Get back on the rocker you've been knocked off of,
get the marksman gloves, hit the weights and figure
shit and keep your sixth sense guarded up.

Fuck the suspense, theatrical elements and tricks,
been thrown your way by phony fucks keeping you
in the shit.

To a point you don't believe in nothing. What the
fuck is love other than lies and a bunch of running?...
a bunch of running, nigga...

Pissed! You've got a middle finger... I mean several,
terrible how nothing you say is considered credible.

You've got a dick for their mouths, and it's edible.
Tell them swallow, spit or ride it, it don't matter, just
don't bite it.

However you choose to slide it, simple or
extravagant, showed your best to muh fuckas and
sours how it went.

Ain't no such thing as soul mates. You've been
replaced by something shiny in the minds of simps
that play shit grimy.

Kindness is a weakness, loyalty ain't shit. You're always there for other people, but they leave you in the pit.

But you're the one that's lunchin' out by displaying common sense ...and nobody gives a fuck, treat you how they see fit.

Gave gold, got dirt. Toilet water, raw sewage from the folks who claim to be the truest.

Instead of flip you keep a stiff upper lip, rarely ever trip or slip and never jumped ship, nigga... never jumped ship, nigga...

Man you're better than this third plant, from the sun. No need to fight, man you already won.

Finished last as the nice guy. It is what it is, but you never hold grudges, so a win is a win.

That's the secret and you know that. Shrug your shoulders Black Atlas, get dead weight up off your back... off your back, nigga...

Wolves travel in packs, but you're the Big Bo$$, Rhino. That's all you need to know, so continue to grow.

Tell them hoes to sit and spin, said it once, say it again. They can kiss your black ass... Like MC Ren.

Shit… let no human dim your grin, fill up your cup. Overflow it with drama or any negative stuff, just chill in the cut. BUT!!!


I'm only just a reflection that sees all, I'm here to keep it realer than anyone you can call.

Spray the Windex, wipe down to make things clear, anytime you need to chit-chat, the mirrors right here…

33

## A1ONE (District Heights Parkway)

I feel like Brad when he asked "is there anybody out here?" Nobody close enough to talk to or otherwise near.

It's clear to me that I was brought into this world alone and for that I don't complain. But the part that troubles me most is that's the way that things have remained.

See… I can maintain a sane frame of mind because my brain is always occupied, but I'm often tied between fantasy, reality and other places where none of these reside.

I abide by the 48 laws, the 33 strategies and all of the seductive arts. In society I do my part to stay on top, but also brace myself for the drop.

Is that a reason to feel alone? Blown from the lessons learned that set a tone in my life from the things that I'm often shown… or not shown even…

Like the love I show for others is hardly ever reflected, so I live my life in a state where I feel neglected. See…

Cause I can always respect it when realness is kept, but being false is an issue that's always inept.

Without all these simple things in my life, I've become numb, cold and downright cynical. Incapable of empathy, down to my last mineral.

That's why my face shows no emotion. Yet I still feel happiness amongst other things, and I seek help in prayer for the blessings that it brings, see...

I'm always on defense mode with my force field always active. No damage can ever vanquish or subside my mind, I've mastered this with practice.

My back is turned to most with a cold shoulder for them to look over. So polar to my molars I can ice skate on Folgers.

As I go through my mind's folders of thoughts of things decayed, these are the reasons I feel alone... I've pushed others away... fuck it...

# Richard & Jasper

These two niggas, wishy-washy unstable, one minute
you cool, the next flipping a table.

One minute you act a fool, the next conversational.
One minute above it all, the next lowest of pitfalls.

Pit stains, when it rains it pours. False confidence,
incoherent incompetent incompetence.

Trustworthy, not really but always there. More
reliable than anyone who claims to care.

Deeply staring at the ceiling trying to figure out this
world, what could make it better while it's spinning
trying not to hurl.

Sometimes an embarrassment, others my best
friends, cool with most of my folks as long as they
have ends.

Helps me to be honest with myself and to others,
takes away my focus and they help me to be noticed.

The life of the party as an uninvited guest, but every
time I come through, I'm rolling with the best.

Social experimentation, labs to run tests, results
imply I needed higher doses, not less.

Should invest in better friendships and quality of
people. Pray more to my father looking up below a
steeple.

Lead and not be mislead by destruction follow sheeple. I'm human, better them than to hang out with a needle.

Won't lead to that exhausted in dire need of peace, but as the saying goes... you're only good as the company you keep...

Waking up in places that I didn't go to sleep. Say and do hurtful things sewing what I reap. Losing many people I would more than love to keep, I've got to, two, too, two...

Complex complexity, simplistic simplicity, nothing makes sense with these levels of intensity.

So confusing I'm just looking for a remedy. Figured out with them, not in need of any sympathy.

Blacking out with a lower form of energy, thinking about friends over time became enemies.

...pretending... but I've got to, too, two, to the two of you...

# Why! (Part Two)

Patience is the message from the Man Upstairs, took some time to understand so now I ain't scared.

Reassurance is a thing for real for reinforcement, now I'm chillin' looking round like worry bout what? Not important.

Had the answers all along, I just had to think deeper, find the right questions for solutions from my keeper.

Had to go through the sleepless nights and misguided energy, torture and mental instability for me to see.

What I was missing and now that I have made peace, ask forgiveness so my blessings ain't blocked and out of reach.

Hold my tongue until it's time to verbalize into speech, silence is golden for now so on that I won't speak.

Glory to the Boss Man helped me find relief, delivered from the torture to my soul and all the grief.

Strengthened my belief to walk on faith and not on facts, pulled me back into transition through miraculous acts...

Why, I know Why so I don't ask why me, mind, heart
and eyes open was blind but now I see.

Thought I was trippin' and wasn't right mentally,
epiphany, moment of clarity made whole instantly...

## Listen Now, Believe Later

*"I couldn't help but notice your pain. It runs deep...*
*SHARE IT WITH ME!!!"* -**Lawrence G. Luckinbill**


I often drift away in silence, prefer to be alone.
Maybe not, but that's the world I've been thrown.

Roll with the punches, go with the flow. Anything
that's cliché is all I've ever known.

Hard worker to the bone, not looking for acceptance.
Easy go but never come is how I've always learned
my lessons, go figure.

Dedicated, simple swallow problems with the liquor.
If I was to go, it'd be one less nigga...

Not suicidal, just a thought that I've been having.
What legacy would be left? Or impact start to
happen?

Nothing left to talk about, only my remains, in the
ground, six feet, life would carry on the same.

Another forgotten souljah in the elements and rain,
and not a soul on earth that understands his pain.

Through his life he had to go against the grain he saw no other way, just to get through day to day in hopes that he can maintain.

*"Listen to me now, believe me later on..."*
**-Khujo Goodie**
...but leave me later on...

## DeadMan's Ballad

He died a while ago for quite a while been gone,
nobody even noticed he was missing til this song.

He was a lost soul misunderstood and written off,
always meant well and tried his best at all costs.

Optimistic but pessimism would beckon,  kept on
stepping in stride his mind was his only weapon.

Against himself and the world crumbling around
him, troubled waters would rise but he can't swim.

A body of the element he claimed could've taken him
out, but I know he wouldn't take that route.

…and he knew he had to face that doubt. Prove to
himself and no one else, what he was about.

He was a soldier in step, with the beat of his own
drum, with urgency he'd handle what would come.

He said fuck it cause he had no other options, made
an object of ridicule, for anyone who's watching.

Destined to be alone he understood early on,
inadvertent hurt he caused by trying to not be wrong.

I don't think that he was selfish at all… but it's hard
to see a great one fall.

Was he strung along or was he the main culprit?
Someone to blame or let be just how you thought it?

He grew tired from being too overwhelmed. Never jumped ship he stood firm but lost control of the helm.

Capsized but stayed cool at the same time, too many things in the deck, that he would rewind.

Resolve was a word to him much too foreign, cause the ones he cared about would always turn and run from him.

Taught to tuck and roll while he's tumbling, and to always rise above what it is that troubles him.

Aimed for the root or lower part of the stem, couldn't find the strength then his eyes grew dim.

Body dropped after one last breath while his mind was still coping, physically stiff and cold, but his eyes stayed open… respect...

## Aperture

It's like I always sing the same ol' song, where in this life did CityRandom go wrong?

I spit the same ol' verse. Same tempo, same pad with the memos, same glass with the Henny, same hi-hats and symbols.

I still kick it with the same negroes, but that ain't problematic til' outsiders start the kicking static.

The panic switch is active, while exercising the tactics of a thinker but off the meter til' the day I meet the reaper.

Same flow, same content, still rhyming bout my nonsense and how I'm mistreated put into context.

It comes off as bitching, but really I need help, but I'm a souljah that possesses extensive knowledge of self.

Not to say I want the wealth cause my health is more important, my family as well but my hearing is so distorted.

My vision ain't 20-20 and I even run from me, when I'm lunchin' out and know I'm on the minds of good company.

My mind is a riot, I'm to silent to be a tyrant. Self-reliant my aspect, with nothing I expect but respect.

Because I give it, preach it, teach it and live it, you can't take it I'm a man who's well aware he has a limit.

Timid? Not at all big dawg in the yard, non issue. That's tough but pass on the tissues and pistols.

Early dismissal or late to arrive, regardless of the standing either way I plan to survive.

Though I collide at times with obstacles, situations and binds, and often visit many places negativity resides.

The dude abides by the laws that came by 48, if you know a few, then maybe we'll relate...

aperture...

## *Haiku*

Couldn't have been my

circle if I was pushed out

so effortlessly...

Chapter Three:

## **<u>Tape Deck Playlist</u>**

*"Music is a therapy to ease the mind"*

### **-Brad "Scarface" Jordan**

A musically influenced trip into my world through my ever changing and open ear to music...

The mini collection of poetry that makes up this chapter are all my life's experiences inspired by and are responses to songs that I've heard and/or often listen to.

# Life Iz Fo Lurnin' Stuff

Inspired By: Life Is For Learning, by Marvin Gaye
and The Artist Pays The Price, by Eightball

*"How do you think it would feel to go around the world in a day?"* -**Eightball**

Now that's a fascinating question there if I must say so Ball. Let me respond with my answer and without one in return. Calculations presume that the speed of sound is roughly 349 meters per second to reach for whom it may concern.

The circumference of the Earth is somewhere around 24,874 miles around at the equator, so at that speed it isn't possible to do because I'd touch down just a tad bit later...

That area's gray, so slightly over a day is when I'd most likely make the specified ETA .

Yeah, my math is all kinds of ridiculous, but I did do a little research to discover something that I was otherwise oblivious.

Almost like I knew what I was talking bout, huh? Sometimes I spew nonsense with little to do about nothing and let my imagination run.

All in good fun and taste, cause life is learning according to what Marvin Gaye say.

*"I'm not a killer, just a poet trying to survive, nigga. Given the choice to ride or die, I chose to ride, nigga. "* -**Eightball**

That was a Premro quotable that reached Maryland from Memphis in 98. Not quite around the world but it's a long way from there to blast out my stereo face.

Factor in the miles I've traveled while listening and sharing something relatable, that's work worth putting in as long as I'm able to.

So it's true that the artist pays the price initially with pieces of their soul to sell, but the audience pays a valid cost as well.

## <u>Your Name...</u>

Inspired By: I Call Your Name, by Switch


A name that slides past my lips... with little to no effort. One that I've called repeatedly that fell on ears that couldn't have become deafer.

Granted, I was reaching... but that's what desperate souls do when they come across one that they just can't bear to lose.

All stops were pulled for what it's worth which amounts to a broken heart and sadness. Rashness when it's not up to me to put an end to all the madness.

Fast is how this life can change or switch up instantly without foresight and warning. From sunset to morning, can't focus through the rain that this cloud over my head is pouring.

Every thought is with you, and in essence particles of me as well. Whether welcomed or not a connection was made that abruptly got derailed.

But still I call your name to no avail… dreaming of what could've been and can't accept that I've failed.

Not just you but myself by allowing something beautiful to go stale. But always held out hope that love would make a way and always prevail.

Maybe that's an old wives tale people tell themselves to fill the void they avoid facing within. Create false realities because it feels so damn good to pretend.

If reality was the dreams I've had, written about and remembered. Analyzed, prayed on and by I've been off centered.

Feeling like a part of me was dismembered, would be the last thing I'd ever figure.

But I suppose that's just how it goes. It's better to have had than not at all I guess… so I call your name once more… then from this I must digress...

GOD bless...

## 2 Da Sky

Inspired by Keep Your Head To The Sky, by Earth, Wind & Fire and No Sunshine, by The Ghetto Twiinz

*"Keep ya head up, keep ya head up for me. Cause the Lord knows he goin make it right ya see.*

*Don't worry bout it trouble comes naturally, don't worry bout it best believe your soul so free, feel me?"* -**Ghetto Twiinz**

GOD given, Heaven sent and GOD blessed. GOD allowed the obstacles in my quest.

Chastised through pain I've been baptized. Time flies while tears fall from my eyes.

Stomach turning do back flips my nerves wrecked. Head up and desperate to find rest.

My days coming though they numbered in this labyrinth, nothing comes easy to those of us who ask for strength.

Relentless, ask questions persistent, still reaching my arms stretched to max length.

Feel cursed but Lord knows know that's not it. Sit still til you reveal what's my gift.

No burden is weight that I can't lift. Aching shins to
my hips for the extent it exists.

It's a reason for the suffering, it's a blessing coming
chill and pop a Bufferin... look up!


*"Keep ya head up, keep ya head up for me. Cause
the Lord knows he goin make it right ya see.*

*Don't worry bout it trouble comes naturally, don't
worry bout it best believe your soul so free, feel
me?"* **-Ghetto Twiinz**

## Friendly Culmination

Inspired By: The End, by The Who

If this is the end… it's so very anticlimactic as closure was never made available as an option, as eventful and suspenseful as things were, it became bittersweet because our destiny was ill fated since the beginning of all time allotted.

Snatched from under my feet was the carpet that had so much potential swept under it. Bumbling blunder, as this crumbling mind wonders stumbling before touching ground as he forcefully lands, it sounds off like the loud crackling of a thunder kick... rumbling.

I'd like to believe that we had electricity, lightning in a bottle... harnessed. But like all energy it needs to be properly free to move about before good things become unstable, stagnant and tarnished.

Like holding on to something that doesn't want to be held on to with a slippery grip, actions speak louder than formed words to pass tongue, gums, teeth and lips.

At least that's what I thought as a showing of my changed behavior, acknowledgment and the sharing of my gifts would represent in favor of meeting or exceeding the standards of a quote, list... unquote.

But long story short... all I'm left with is opportunity missed... cut throat...

I was taught Love is supposed to breed, not shun, not be treated as a loaded gun, cocked, aimed or weaponized with the beam masterfully placed between the eyes of the other with intent to leave them dead where they lie and try to show the other otherwise.

But it's all cause and effect and how people project with what they have and leave because of what's in them they by all means must protect.

Whatever that means but, understood... Respect!

In other words, if it ain't working for you or ain't worth working it out or working through, do what you gotta do to live your truth. I'll peacefully move aside to leave you to make your moves...

So handle them... do your thing and what you do, slim... it's cool...

## Sheriff Road NE.

Inspired By: Street Life, by Scarface

The intoxicating aroma of gun smoke puts my nose on sensory overload at the top of the AM. While seeing few people on their way to work at jobs that go out of their way to under pay them.

Unfulfilled and barely inspired by self-interests but purely out of necessity... suited and booted. For homes that they can barely afford or support and mouths they have to feed... but somebody's gotta do it...

People heading in and out like old school Metrobus transfers, red, in and out, blue... To do and get to where they need to be to make their little, small time, minimum wage... loot.

...scratch... But then there's the folks out of and in plain sight across the street doing what they do to make due while bagging up and filling clear valves quickly moving what I guess is a brand new batch.

Slang and serve is their ambitious or not so much mission to rid themselves of destructive product. With no regard to the community and the functional people and children of it who might care and are left to deal with such misconduct.

Definitely a way to get by if viewed from both sides of the spectrum as the motto "get it how you live" comes to a mind unclosed. Whether punching a clock or posted on the block non stop a grind is a grind, it is what it is, I suppose.

With my underage, adolescent, unsuspecting... prepubescent, bright, brown eyes within this setting... from the second floor window I've witnessed things that's much too common with folks of my complexion.

PGC MD was literally right across the other street but being as that we was right on the border it looked no different. What I thought was the other side of the tracks was walking distance and in eye shot of this apartment window that I sit in.

What's the lesson is a question I ask while reminiscing this elaborate, yet vague recollection. I guess at that time in my life I was and to this day remain unaffected.

I have my moms to thank for that because she was one of those few folks who stepped over the used up needles, plenty of mini empty zip baggies, shell casings and shards of shattered glass pipes to make it to that bus stop to provide my big brother and I what little we had, but was enough to gain some type of momentum and insight in this life.

My aunt was always there, and pops... he was probably drunk somewhere who knows where in this neighborhood of modern day ruins. That built this young man's character at entry level in a world that doesn't care who you are and what you may be pursuing.

For some it's an illusion because the very thought of doing better brings to their faces blank stares and looks of confusion. To them that's delusion that has them consuming their narcotic of choice not reducing but including more to what substance they're using and abusing.

Trying to get through personal anguish, pain and suffering or simply to perpetuate a euphoric state from a party that's long over. Strung out thin to places of no return as the monkeys on their backs react to not having their desired exposure.

Who am I to ever look down the bridge of my young nose and pass any type of judgement on those getting by. High or showboating, flexing muscle with whatever side piece or big guns they toting.

All victims of circumstance who are taking whatever chance or opportunities afforded, maybe... But this is the norm that my lil' six, seven or eight year old mind processes frequently, almost daily...

poor baby...

## Unfamiliar (Used Ta Know Ya)

Inspired by: Somebody That I Used To Know, by Gotye and a random meme I saw on Facebook.

How should I feel? I don't feel shit. Remember… you left me. So anti this guy, what he stood for, what he offered all that shit wasn't worth a damn so you went where you wanted to be.

Cool and the gang, ain't no thang, trippin' is for lames and I ain't one of those cause from that ain't nuffin' to gain fuck my effort and pain that's against YOUR grain.

Cool hand icy soul, how I been since conceived in that in March of 83. My outlook on life was preconceived for the man that I was meant to be.

The fuck I look like trying to dis or not acknowledge my part in all that bullshit. To roll out is what you saw fit.

When I was in the pit ain't mean shit… Why you reach out?…To rekindle something you figured you had missed?

I'd be a liar if I said I still didn't have love, with me that shit ain't easily lost or left behind. When I say shit, I mean shit when said raw spit and un refined.

I created opportunity and you created a bind… at least in my eyes. Not neglecting what I presented to you but your mind works differently than mine.

Straight get back… you're one of those… or am I giving myself too much credit? It all boils down to the root which is something I did in which I regretted.

That's people I guess... different strokes for different folks. Held my chin up, and accepted what's coming then you suddenly caught ghost.

Why did you come back? Why do you so called care? What do you want? Tried to be all ears and feel you cause a respectful, generous, gentleman is how I was raised and how I behave, and it's not in me to stunt.

Showed me I wasn't shit without muttering a single word. Again… cool and the gang so what's done is done and left with the birds.

Who's looking unfamiliar? I'm still the same person but wiser and far removed. No stranger danger or anything that implies an attitude or me outright being rude.

Fuck me though... I accepted that. So… why you even come back? To rub in my face your new life and make excuses for how you chose to react?

I take it all as rational. No apologies to me are necessary, wanted or even asked for. It just wasn't real... Not excusing my actions or what I did to break the deal.

I just thought everything meant more or at the very least something. But I'm an over thinker and that doesn't keep those I care about from running... now tell me something...

# The Raft

Inspired By: Sail, by AWOL Nation

The wind is too strong, there's a hole in my sail. The
current rough, but still I prevail.

Sick of the pain and taking the blame for mistakes of
others with infinite gain. My people are struggling,
hurting and starving, judged by a system that makes
us their targets.

My raft is sinking, unnatural battle. My oars are gone
I'm up the creek without a paddle.

It's babies crying. Pacifier, bottle, rattle, treat us like
sheep to lead the weak then slaughter off like cattle.

Saddle up, the others are spurs their backs, the
hunters have made them their prey. Living life in
these conditions we trapped in why wouldn't you try
to get away?

## Ice Cream Social Media Status Studies Experiment (Vada Sultenfuss)

Inspired by Ice Cream, by JS and Ice Cream, by Raekwon of The Wu Tang Clan


What's my favorite flavor? Chocolate, caramel, butter pecan, mix breed neapolitan, something with a swirl? Froze til I warm it up off the scoop when in my hands and out the barrel.

Homemade to capture that perfect taste and texture. Mixed all the right ingredients to perfection no flexing, churned and stirred with little to no pressure.

Soft serve you at first before sprinkles I taste the cherry. Pull the stem and then the whipped cream cums naturally when I make it ready.

Face first no utensils, certified with credentials. Beard Gang soaked from how you melted through the bowl as if what I pulled off was monumental.

I possess more than potential. It's my harnessed skill that made you feel that and want seconds or more and make you wanna get this sundae banana peeled.

But it's all about you right now. Sit back, chill and I'll make you make the mess. Crush cookies and all your goodies, and you ain't even had my best...

# The End Result

Inspired by Bulletproof Soul, by Sade

*"I was so in love with you. You rarely see a love that's true.*

*Wasn't that enough for you? Wasn't that enough for you?*

*I would climb a mountain. I wouldn't want to see you fall.*

*Rock climb for you, and give you a reason for it all..."* **-Sade**

Ain't, nuffin' and wouldn't are the operative word in this discussion. Ain't nuffin' that I wouldn't have done to keep you blushing.

Ain't nuffin' that I wouldn't have done to feel you touching. Ain't nuffin' that I wouldn't have done to know you loving... me...

Far from perfect I gave all I had to give. A life with me you didn't see and didn't want to live.

I probably wanted someone that never belonged to me. So you took back what you offered so mostly I let you be.

Thought we had a future, and that, I had belief in.
But sleeping get's you caught late so Frank cut out
all the dreaming.

Ain't no love been  lost, and ain't nobody beefing.
Ain't nobody bitter or jumping off of the deep end.

I was reaching when I tried to rebuild what you was
leaving, but people change and so does life the
universe be teaching.

I wore it on my sleeve just to prove, and to show you
that there wasn't a mountain I wouldn't move.

If there ever was a do over would I have told the
truth? Or pacify a lie that would've grew to
something fluke?

It's understood you hit the roof for the reasons that
you decided, so the dude abided raised his chin and
kept on climbing.

Thought I would meet you at the summit or peak,
plant a flag and flaunt it. Made yourself out of reach
off to what you really wanted.

Not I, so I waved bye falling to the Earth, ropes cut,
no foothold, nuffin' I could do would work... but I
tried anyway...

*"I was so in love with you. You rarely see a love that's true.*

*Wasn't that enough for you? Wasn't that enough for you?*

*I would climb a mountain. I wouldn't want to see you fall.*

*Rock climb for you, and give you a reason for it all..."* **-Sade**

## _Haiku_

Don't hit my phone just

leave me lone and get used to

hearing the dial tone...

Chapter Four:

## PROpul(l)SHUN

Pro /prō/ (noun) an advantage of something or an argument in favor of a course of action.

Pull /po͝ol/ (verb) (informal) move one's body in a specified direction, especially against resistance.

Shun /SHən/ (verb) persistently avoid, ignore, or reject (someone or something) through antipathy or caution.

The content of this chapter include pieces based on prayers, introspective moments that I've had and reminders of what I already have and know of within. Could they possibly hold the answers and solutions to what I've asked and waited for? Hmmmm…

## Why! (The Conclusion)

Why, I know Why so I don't ask why me. Mind, heart and eyes open was blind but now I see.

Thought I was trippin' and wasn't right mentally. Epiphany, moment of clarity made whole instantly...

Why in this context is not a question. It's me understanding what it all means and knowing my reflection.

All things come full circle to completion with patience, so if it's meant to be and real, hope you don't mind waiting.

So I don't ask "why?", because I know the cause and effect, the Source came direct and showed me what it is that I must protect.

Whatever the test, storm, season or vision quest... pay attention. The clues are there to use to help you rise up above the mess.

Why has now become a statement, to give me purpose and motivation until I reach my placement.

All the things I'm faced with is preparation for the end game. Things change and so do people... stay in your lane... or come out of it... WHY!...

Why, I know Why so I don't ask why me. Mind,
heart and eyes open was blind but now I see.

Thought I was trippin' and wasn't right mentally.
Epiphany, moment of clarity made whole instantly...

## Rags To This…

I'm the son of a gas station attendant, and the son of a mother who's independence. Molded a man who's will to go the distance with anything centered around rebellion and resistance.

Latch key variety is me, born in 83, native of DC.

Typical stories of Payless shoe trips, Morton's, Woolworth, and them Discount Mart fits.

Played Nintendo, watched TV. Wasn't into homework, watched TV.

Played with Thunder Cats, He Man and Mr. T, dish liquid bubble bath, 9 o'clock went to sleep.

I'm the baby brother of an asshole. I'm the little cuz of bigger assholes. But they're the ones who took the runt and formed a mold and I love them all to death for that I mean it from my soul.

I'm a nephew, I'm a grandson. Godfather, good friend don't think I missed none.

Not a husband, no kids of my own at the moment I'm just cool with being grown, and living on my own.

Not complacent, not at all, no sir! Just working on having a better way with words.

All the bull, you could feed it to the birds. Fall back and be observant, watch the soup spoon stir.

Greatness awaits for those who's patient. I'm too anxious, so keep the wait list.

(Jada)Kiss said the game needs a face-lift, well I'm not the one to give it so it's cool to hate this.

Just making songs to fill up my playlist, build my catalog on inconsistent basis.

Things could be worse, like being caged in some steel bracelets, but I'm blessed and favored, GOD's graces...

Went from rags to this. Still ain't rich, still ain't rich, still ain't rich.

Got a talent chose not to waste it... but I'm blessed and favored, GOD's graces...

## An Incontrovertible Contemplation

All that was heard was death when I tried to speak life, kept me in the dark when I tried to bring light.

Can admit to being wrong and be humble when I'm right, if you wanna go, be gone you might be better out my life.

Paid dues for irreconcilable issues, harsh truth is I worked to see it through with you.

But that missed you... somehow that missed you...


I ask for nothing unreasonable if for anything at all. This closed mouth stays fed because I feed myself substantially to the point it looks like greed to others on the other side of the two way mirrored wall.

You'd rather me fall than fly so why should I waste my time trying to have pride in and rise to the expectations of those who don't hide while blatantly attempting to tear me down bare faced with no disguise?

Fool me once... that's just a George W. Bush shame, point blank period. If that's the intent going in I wasn't even from the gate ever taken serious.

So that's my fault for not recognizing while having my third eye blinded by optimism while trying to always keep things in the perspective of positivity in a positive place positively, totally discrediting the possibility that my best interests face neglect and ingest what I let in based on the parameters that I set.

Comes off as low standards and or self esteem, huh? Not the case ever, just decided to experiment with trying something different by allowing others in and attempting to see the good they may possess under the surface under places there may very well just be none.

I go hard because I have to. Based on the options I'm presented I should be in a perpetual down mood, nah, walk a couple steps keep your mile in my shoes would be more than enough to make you stressed, frustrated and want to cry too.

But I'm a man and rather than get emotional or show and expose weakness, I go harder and grow colder to continue to carry Black Atlas' boulder known as the Earth on my shoulders until what I go through is over.

Some call it insanity while I argue responsibility. Only I as me should bear the weight and step up to face, face to face the world I occupy properly handling in my unorthodox, unconventional manner to make good on every possibility.

Realized it's hip to be square because this L 7 observes parallel right angles to bring forth peace and awareness, and not have my words taken and twisted as finesse or willing to compete in competitions that display no vision and disregard the fact that things should be operated and done in all fairness.

Clearly I'm alone in that thought process and theory, but if only negativity and nothing else is put back in me, forgive me for being leery... or don't, really...

But all l that was heard was death when I tried to speak life, kept me in the dark when I tried to bring light.

Can admit to being wrong and be humble when I'm right, if you wanna go, be gone you might be better out my life.

Paid dues for irreconcilable issues, harsh truth is I worked to see it through with you.

Can't be mad at, anything a soul refuse, bread crumbs to three course meals served... all of that to not even be heard...

Know better than to go where not wanted and to assume, anything about another who pushed you out of their room.

But that missed you... how'd that miss you?... true...

# Transitional Psyche (Inner G)

Woe is me… no it ain't, growth is me, so hopefully the man you see is posted where he's supposed to be.

Front man on top and took the lead, natural nutrients nurtured this seed, roots broke the earth through concrete and steel beams to bear fruit for all to feed.

For those who hunger for more... be it wisdom, knowledge and strength... myself included. At times I need all of these so my refuge is with me in places secluded.

Cleanse the palate of contamination and things otherwise polluted. Vaccinate the hate and remedy all that's become convoluted.

It's a new day so let's leave the problems of the past where they lay, or take advantage of this clean slate to right the wrongs and uncover truths to see the outcome of in which things play.

Control what's controllable, and do what's doable. Experience something new to you mind over matter discover what is suitable.

Next move the best move step up to what tests you, GOD blessed you with tools how to use… it's up to you.

## An Introspective Moment

*"You do not need to know precisely what is happening, or where it is all going. What you need is to recognize the possibilities and challenges offered by the present moment, and to embrace them with courage, faith and hope..."* -**Thomas Merton**

***FreeMan:*** Nothing is what it seems...
***Big Bo$$ Rhino:*** **What you mean?**
Been having some weird dreams that snap me from my sleep.

Can't tell the difference of what to believe, cause sometimes they are messages or warnings, got me up all times of the morning.

Restless is my soul...

**Frank, you just be overthinking, it's good to be prepared for things so stop reaching.**

**Shift your focus to what's next or best to make a come up. Tomorrow's a new day, just wait until the sun's up.**

I know, but the Black Atlus... struggles with letting go, accepting what he already knows.

Be it detriment or something making room for something better, trouble on my mind ignored to get myself together.

That ain't right, you must explore, the depths. Get to the bottom til peace feels like death.

In a sense of no worries, thoughts clear not blurry, take your time with life be careful there's no hurry.

...but what about the signs and dreams that I've seen? Shown way too vividly, clear and pristine?

Look, whatever's meant to be... just let it. GOD speaks volumes trust him, you won't regret it.

With him, you made it this far but you can go farther. Keep your head up by nothing else you should be bothered.

Moved or uprooted... but encouraged. Strengthened, made better... now flourish...

**<u>Give it up to GOD... NOW FLOURISH!!!</u>**

# Life's Incertitude

These liquor bottles fill the void of, something I'm
not seeing. Something I'm not getting, something that
I'm not believing.

Something that was told to me I'm soon to be
receiving, though I claim it in the universe the same
things keep repeating.

It's a method to the madness and there always is
message, on lookout for the lessons make it worth the
time invested.

Can't end up in a place where I missed or blocked my
blessings, so ask for confirmation in these prayer
filled sessions.

Sometimes, the reply is… vocal. Other times through
dreams, others through actions intervened.

Other times through people or the places that I end
up in, always mind blowing when I realize what I'm
witnessing.

I talk slow because I don't know who's listening, who could offer something pitching in or add to simp shit.

Maybe someone can relate agree or disagree, or am I overthinking things that aim to keep me from my peace…

*"I believe that I am not responsible for the meaningfulness or meaninglessness of life, but that I am responsible for what I do with the life I've got."*

**-Hermann Hesse**

What is the dream that I'm chasing in particular, thinking bout it broken down to levels that's molecular.

Rise to all occasions and not settle as the victim of, take my thoughts and free them on these pads I keep em' written up.

Overflowing, like where's it all going, better question how I'm getting there to harvest what I'm growing.

Reaping what I'm sewing planting seeds that's beneficial, not just for me but everybody that's on my team official.

Been, the inside joke or punchline, like everybody's in on something that I'm not, STOP!!!

Cut the bullshit, let me make my music, leave me be to fly alone and see who I influence.

Things is wild and I don't even know what I be doing, I said this all before like broken records, a nuisance.

Probably overlooking facts ignoring what the truth is, no one else to blame if I'm the one who's being stupid...

*"The meaning of life is not an unquestionable answer; it is an unanswerable question."*

**-Terri Guillemets**

Our father... who put me in this game as a starter, who kept me lifted up even at times I wouldn't bother.

Who knows and understands my intricate details inside and out and when I give resistance pulls me back and holds me harder.

I may not always pass your tests but I try my best with my human comprehension to take a seat and rest because it's known that you have it all under control. That's what I believe and I'm told, but it's hard to sit back idle waiting to watch your plan unfold.

Patience is a virtue passed on by spirits from and of you. As well as strength, peace, mercy, forgiveness and for all of that and more I'm thankful.

I'm still a fool at times and will always fall short of the praise, glory and grace you deserve and possess, but through it all you've carried or walked beside and continued to keep me blessed... so why should I be stressed?...

*"MEANING OF LIFE: TO SHINE A LIGHT WHERE THERE IS NO LIGHT AND TAKE RESPONSIBILITY FOR SHINING THAT LIGHT."*

**-Noelani Musicaro**

## Room TEMPERature

If you a Pac fan, how'd you feel when he dropped blasphemy? Or when Pastor T dropped Vica Versa just to see where your mind would be?

Me? My firm belief stands firm, unbothered and unswayed, because I know who in which my sins were paid on the table laid flat and in the open where all my demons should, can, would and will be slayed.

This book of my life is full of pages that should be by this time far behind and long distant. Like a relative that you hear from long distance few and far between because they ain't heard from you in a while but... in any instance...

Talk, or try to talk like... "Hello"... followed by a long uneasy breeze or gust of dead air and silence for what feels like hours, but it's only been a few seconds... to ask for something or come off reckless is what I'm expecting while on guard with weapons, ready at my disposal because I know that at any point left is the direction bound to be went.

Evident that the problem lies within he, she, thyself, somebody else... hell... me. But to the wielder of the Sword of Omens' Eye of Thundera sight beyond sight is properly given to the one who isn't sleep.

Play the game or present it like Jigsaw fair but all in, doubled down, balls deep and be there ready to be in it to win it for keeps. Learn to doggy paddle or at least tread water if you end up in the deeper shittier, shittiest end of shit's creek.

Realign my energy so it's seen that I'm bigger than the drama, illegitimate beef, and loose talk that I heard through third parties that said they heard someone downwardly speak or with me would not meet. I often turn the other cheek, or not so, but mostly easily forgive and could give a damn about irrelevant opinions of those who may or may not think I'm weak and over it all while in such a position to not lose a single, solitary wink of sleep.

I'd rather raise my fist partially clenched with two fingers released and up in a "V" as symbolism to have and offer peace so we all can win, but the same hand can be turned around with the index lowered and what's left is where any hateful, hate fuled, back end mule faced commode tool, disgraceful soul can sit and spin...

*"Thank you! Come again!"* -**Apu**
**Nahasapeemapetilon**

## Could Be...

Could be worse, could be a lot better, not complaining cause no one listens just get your shit together.

Glass empty or is it full of air. Dead silence is all that's there nothing else compares.

Sit alone in a lit room til it's dark and no light comes through the windows, not a clue of what to do to make it through so I grab a pillow.

Lay my head down and toss and turn as the thoughts keep rushing. Good or bad I explore it all to find purpose and what I'm not touching.

Some things probably best left alone but I've never been a coward. Never have I been one of those that run from trouble regardless of how high it towers.

Plastic bag in a breeze, taken away with such ease, gone wherever the wind please, til it gets stuck in a tree.

What's the next move I ask myself so steps can be taken. Full and not half or backwards, move away from bad factors.

Could be worse, could be a lot better, make due with what's in front of me now, make official to the letter.

## Cellf Centered

Notebooks, pads and pens have become my most relatable friends as a clean slate constructed for creation as a place where the unlimited possibilities never end.

Fade to black in the deepest depths of my subconscious, discover and forcefully uncover truths and skills worth the time, work and effort to harness.

Bring it all to the surface uncovered though nervous, push forward with it anyway unafraid but with courage encouraged by what's GOD given to expose my purpose.

MY LORD...

If there's a lesson learned, nothing you go through is worthless. Though overwhelmed by what hurt is, small victories serve as the healthy distraction from all that by creating helpful and motivational diversions.

It's cool to sit alone in that four cornered room staring at candles. Flip the switches on your panel, and adjust what it is and/or isn't that you're willing to handle.

Preview, sample, save in your que for later review, what works for me may not work for you so continue... by all means, do what you do.

I'm a conqueror on my own and about myself I own that. Mathematically I'm four and eight so no matter what I'm straight, can't debate my upcoming greatness because I've been shown that...

Now tell me... how you love that?

## A Written Prayer

Our father... who put me in this game as a starter, who kept me lifted up even at times I wouldn't bother.

Who knows and understands my intricate details inside and out and when I give resistance pulls me back and holds me harder.

I may not always pass your tests but I try my best with my human comprehension to take a seat and rest because it's known that you have it all under control, that's what I believe and I'm told... but it's hard to sit back idle waiting to watch your plan unfold.

Patience is a virtue passed on by spirits from and of you... as well as strength, peace, mercy, forgiveness and for all of that and more I'm thankful.

I'm still a fool at times and will always fall short of the praise, glory and grace you deserve and possess, but through it all you've carried or walked beside and continued to keep me blessed... so why should I be stressed?

Thank You.


AMEN

## Salud

This is a dedication to those of you who sustained the cold and stuck with me in the fold, to find my footing on this road and provided enough warmth to thaw this icy soul.

All that glitters ain't gold... by now at this point I know better than that, but prepared for attack against anything that stands in the way of everything that I had to reattach.

Fix what I lacked while being patient and when it came back unfamiliar and looking different, that's the work of GOD revealing to me that what he wants for my life is not too distant.

Pay attention and don't be a mark or sucker, my behind has been exposed enough to those whose lips I told to keep puckered and tired from their energy that had me outwardly tuckered.

Moved on and ain't about that life no more but I'll probably speak on it from time to time but less frequently, because ain't no grudges held and it's cool to live a life free of enemies.

I've rediscovered love and it now fosters a new definition, now... for whom it concerns and who it deserves to be shared with and given to I'm cautious with it but how, where and when given it's done with the best of my ability and greatest of intentions...
SALUD...

# Honest To GOD

Lord... I wanna talk to you but don't know what to say after expressing my gratitude... so I'll just shoot. Help me to correct my attitude and become a man in better moods.

You've been more than graceful and merciful... I'm thankful but don't at all feel purposeful.

Time reveals all according to your plan, Jusme repeatedly beat that into the mind of this Free, Man's mind that it's yours and not mine.

So I try to stay aware and prepare for what you allow to come... but what is it? I've asked and received little to no response or inkling of what it is or isn't.

It becomes harder to hold on to faith while watching and waiting, but I'll never neglect to remember that one moment you quietly spoke "be patient."

That's all you said so... what should I be expecting? I try my best to do as you say but this here is one tough lesson.

Did I misunderstand you or was it not you who spoke at all? I shouldn't question but my back's against the wall.

At one point I became so observant to everything because I didn't want to nor could afford to miss your call. What I thought was you I'm unsure if it was and what felt right turned out to be wrong.

Is it something I missed? Something I'm not doing? Someplace I'm not going?... Something I'm not hearing or seeing? Something I'm ignoring?

I often pray for your leadership and guidance so your light can show the way. I understand your will is perfect but I feel ignored and left to make mistakes.

But I also pray for strength and I get how that works. Comparable to weight lifting, no pain no gain before better it oftentimes get's worse.

Maybe I still have to be patient for something else because your plan has yet to be fulfilled. So until revealed please be a shield to protect while I sit still...

## Remember My Name

This is me attempting to achieve immortality. By listening to this you've been made a witness of the FreeMan's trails, small to great victories and triumphs overcome and endured with extreme vitality.

After I'm dead and gone eternally sleep and body buried 6 feet deep in a cemetery plot decaying and left to rot. Though not free of blemishes or scot and work put in to shoot my shot, the name I left behind may not be a lot, but it's all to give I've got....

### _Haiku_

If I'm able to

walk away not owing a

thing, I'm good. Debts paid...

# BONUS TRACK

# Lost & Found Luv

A tale of triumph and discovery, somebody sound the trumpets for me… toot my own horn cause I worked hard to gain this glory.

All the highs and lows crashed the boards to equalize through tough times, and face my demons swept away with rising tides I stand with pride.

Not out the woods yet but there's a view, opening. Ask the Lord what should I do, what weapons I should use?

The faint smell of success is getting stronger, so it's not too much longer for something tangibles in the palm of.

This cool hand my icy soul's a little warmer, partially thawed and frost bit… but hot for those that's in my corner.

Thanks a lot for obstacles, I needed that. I always pray for strength and GOD the brightest where my weakness at.

Pat on the back for me, from me. Wiped my own tears on my own sleeve.

I'm Eddie Grant because now I see clearly. I'm better now than I was before and healed from all that's silly.

Sky's the limit so I focus on it's beauty, make it my duty to reach what I've seen profusely.

Turned why into a statement not a question to be asked. Studied did the footwork and discovered what would last.

Follow and trust a GOD that's more than able. Get up and walk away leave burdens at the table.

Been unstable and unbalance for a while now, forgiveness is divine I rise to put it down.

I needed love so I put myself above all, and where I didn't get it off a lot of folks would fall.

To those who survived, I say on record just for y'all…

# I'm indebted till my dying day and always I'm on call!!!

www.ingramcontent.com/pod-product-compliance
Lightning Source LLC
LaVergne TN
LVHW051419080426
835508LV00022B/3161